"MASTER HAROLD"
. . . and the boys

A DRAMA

by
Athol Fugard

SAMUEL FRENCH, INC.
45 West 25th Street   NEW YORK 10010
7623 Sunset Boulevard HOLLYWOOD 90046
LONDON   TORONTO

for Sam and H.D.F.

"MASTER HAROLD" . . . and the boys

. . . opened on Broadway May 4, 1982, at the Lyceum Theatre. The cast was as follows:

SAM .... Zakes Mokae
WILLIE .... Danny Glover
HALLY .... Lonny Price

The production was directed by the author. Costumes were by Sheila McLamb; scenery by Jane Clark; lighting by David Noling; stage movement by Wesley Fata.

The original Yale Repertory Theatre production was produced on Broadway by the Shubert Organization, Freydburg-Bloch Productions, Dasha Epstein, Emanuel Azenberg and David Geffen.

SPECIAL MUSIC ROYALTY NOTE:

For amateurs, music royalty is $5.00 per performance. For stock productions, music royalty quoted upon application. Music royalty is for the use of the songs "Little Man, You've Had a Busy Day" and "You're the Cream in My Coffee." which must be used in production of "MASTER HAROLD" . . . AND THE BOYS.

"MASTER HAROLD"
. . . and the boys

by
Athol Fugard

The St. Georges Park Tea Room on a wet and windy Port Elizabeth afternoon.

> *Tables and chairs have been cleared and are stacked on one side except for one which stands apart with a single chair. On this table a knife, fork, spoon and side-plate in anticipation of a simple meal together with a pile of comic books. Other elements: a serving counter with a few stale cakes under glass and a not-very-impressive display of sweets, cigarettes and cool-drinks etc.; a few cardboard advertising handouts — Cadbury's Chocolate, Coca-cola — and a blackboard on which an untrained hand has chalked up the prices of Tea, Coffee, Scones, Milkshakes — all flavours — and Cool-drinks; a few sad ferns in pots; a telephone; an old-style jukebox. There is an entrance on one side and an exit into a kitchen on the other.*

Leaning on the solitary table, his head cupped in one hand as he pages through one of the comic books, is SAM. A black man in his late thirties. He wears the white coat of a waiter. Behind him on his knees, mopping down the floor with a bucket of water and a rag, is WILLIE. Also black and about the same age as SAM. He has his sleeves and trousers rolled up.

The year: 1950.

WILLIE. *(singing as he works)*
SHE WAS SCANDALISIN MY NAME
CALLED IT LOVE BUT WAS PLAYIN' A GAME
SHE CALLED ME HONEY; SHE TOOK MY MONEY–
(He gets up and moves the bucket; stands and sings.)
SHE WAS SCANDALIZIN MY NAME...
(Thinking for a moment, then raising his arms to hold an imaginary partner, he launches into an intricate ballroom dance step. Although a mildly comic figure he reveals a reasonable degree of accomplishment.) Hey Sam.

(SAM, absorbed in the comic book does not respond.)

WILLIE. Hey Boet Sam!

(SAM looks up.)

WILLIE. I'm getting it. The Quickstep. Look now and tell me. *(He repeats the step.)* Well?
SAM. *(He wasn't concentrating.)* Show me again.
WILLIE. Okay, count for me.

SAM. Ready?

WILLIE. Ready.

SAM. A-n-d one two three four ... and one two three four ... Relax, Willie!

WILLIE. *(desperate but still dancing)* I am relax.

SAM. No you're not.

WILLIE. *(He falters.)* Ag no man, Sam! Mustn't talk. You make me make mistakes.

SAM. But you're too stiff.

WILLIE. Yesterday I'm not straight .... today I'm too stiff!

SAM. Well you are. You asked me and I'm telling you.

WILLIE. Where?

SAM. Everywhere. Try to glide through it.

WILLIE. What's this — glide?

SAM. Ja, make it smooth. And give it more style. It must look like you're enjoying yourself.

WILLIE. *(emphatically)* I wasn't.

SAM. Exactly.

WILLIE. How can I enjoy myself? Not straight, too stiff and now it's also glide, give it more style, make it smooth .... Haai! Is hard to remember all those things Boet Sam.

SAM. That's your trouble. You're trying too hard.

WILLIE. I try hard because it *is* hard.

SAM. But don't let me see it. The secret is to make it look easy. Ball room must look happy Willie, not like hard work. It must .... Ja! ... it must look like romance.

WILLIE. Now another one! What's this romance?

SAM. Love story with happy ending. A handsome man

in tails, and in his arms, smiling at him, a beautiful lady in evening dress!

WILLIE. Fred Astaire Ginger Rogers.

SAM. You got it. Tapdance or Ballroom, it's the same. Romance. In two weeks' time when the judges look at you and Hilda they must see a man and woman *who are* dancing their way to a happy ending. What I saw was you holding her like you were frightened she was going to run away.

WILLIE. Ja! Because that is what she wants to do! I got no romance left for Hilda anymore, Boet Sam.

SAM. Then pretend. When you put your arms around Hilda, imagine she is Ginger Rogers.

WILLIE. With no teeth? You try.

SAM. Well just remember, there's only two weeks left.

WILLIE. I know, I know! *(to the jukebox)* I do it better with music. You got sixpence for Sarah Vaughan?

SAM. That's a slow foxtrot. You're practising the quickstep.

WILLIE. I'll practise slow foxtrot.

SAM. *(shaking his head)* It's your turn to put money in the jukebox.

WILLIE. I only got busfare to go home. *(He returns disconsolately to his work.)* Ginger Rogers! Love story and happy ending! She's doing it alright, Boet Sam, but is not me she's giving happy endings. Fokin Hoar! Three nights now she doesn't come practise. I wind-up gramaphone, I get record ready and I sit and wait. What happens? Nothing. Ten o'clock I start dancing with my pillow. You try and practise this romance by yourself, Boet Sam. Struesgod, she doesn't come tonight, I take back my dress and ballroom shoes and I find me new partner. Size twenty-six. Shoes size seven. ... And now she's also making trouble for me with the baby again. Reports me to child Wellfed, that I'm not giving her money. She lies! Every week I am giving her money for milk. And how do I know is my baby? Only his hair looks like me. She's fucking around all the time I turn my back. Hilda Samuels is a bitch! *(pause)* Hey Sam!

SAM. Ja.

WILLIE. You listening?

SAM. Ja.

WILLIE. So what you say?

SAM. About Hilda?

WILLIE. Ja.

SAM. When did you last give her a hiding?

WILLIE. *(reluctantly)* Sunday night.

SAM. And today is Thursday.

WILLIE. *(He knows what's coming.)* Okay.

SAM. Hiding on Sunday night, than Monday, Tuesday and Wednesday she doesn't come to practise ... and you are asking me why?

WILLIE. I said okay, Boet Sam!

SAM. You hit her too much. One day she's going to leave you for good.

WILLIE. So? She makes me the hell-in too much.

SAM. *(emphasizing his point)* *Too* much and *too* hard. You had the same trouble with Eunice.

WILLIE. Because she also make the hell-in, Boet Sam. She never got the steps right. Even the waltz.

SAM. Beating her up every time you make a mistake in

the waltz? *(shaking his head)* No, Willie! That takes the pleasure out of ballroom dancing.

WILLIE. Hilda is not too bad with the waltz, Boet Sam. Is the quickstep where the trouble starts.

SAM. *(teasing him gently)* How's your pillow with the quickstep?

WILLIE. *(ignoring the tease)* Good! And why? Because it got no legs. That's her trouble. She can't move them quick enough, Boet Sam. I start the record and before halfway Count Basie is already winning. Only time we catch-up with him is when gramaphone runs down. *(SAM laughs.)* Haaikona Boet Sam, is not funny.

SAM. *(snapping his fingers)* I got it! Give her a handicap.

WILLIE. What's that?

SAM. Give her a ten-second start and then let Count Basie go. Then I put my money on her. Hot favourite in the Ballroom Stakes: Hilda Samuels ridden by Willie Malopo.

WILLIE. *(turning away)* I'm not talking to you no more.

SAM. *(relenting)* Sorry, Willie...

WILLIE. It's finish between us.

SAM. Okay okay ... I'll stop.

WILLIE. You can also fok-off.

SAM. Willie, listen! I want to help *you*!

WILLIE. No more jokes?

SAM. I promise.

WILLIE. Okay. Help me.

SAM. *(his turn to hold an imaginary partner)* Look and learn. Feet together. Back straight. Body relaxed. Right hand placed gently in the small of her back and wait for the music. Don't start worrying about making mistakes or about the judges or the other competitors. It's just you, Hilda and the music and you're going to have a good time. What Count Basie do you play?

WILLIE. You're the cream in my coffee; you're the salt in my stew.

SAM. Right. Give it to me in strict tempo.

WILLIE. Ready?

SAM. Ready.

WILLIE. A-n-d ... *(singing)*
YOU'RE THE CREAM IN MY COFFEE;
YOU'RE THE SALT IN MY STEW.
YOU WILL ALWAYS BE MY NECESSITY;
I'D BE LOST WITHOUT YOU;
YOU'RE THE STARCH IN MY COLLAR;
YOU'RE THE LACE IN MY SHOE.
YOU WILL ALWAYS BE MY NECESSITY;
I'D BE LOST WITHOUT YOU.

(While WILLY sings, SAM launches into the quickstep. He is obviously a much more accomplished dancer than WILLY. HALLY enters. He is a 17-year old white boy, wearing a wet raincoat and carrying a school case. He stops and watches SAM. The demonstration comes to an end with a flourish of applause from HALLY and WILLY.)

HALLY. Bravo! No question about it. First place goes to Mr. Sam Semela.

WILLIE. *(in total agreement)* You was gliding with style, Baet Sam.

HALLY. *(cheerfully)* How's it chaps?

SAM. Okay Hally.

WILLIE. *(springing to attention like a soldier and saluting)* At your service, Master Harold!

SAM. Not long to the big event, hey!

SAM. Two weeks.

HALLY. You nervous?

SAM. No.

HALLY. Think you stand a chance?

SAM. Let's just say I'm ready to go out there and dance.

HALLY. It looked like it. What about you, Willie? *(WILLIE groans.)* What's the matter?

SAM. He's got leg trouble.

HALLY. *(innocently)* Oh, sorry to hear that, Willie.

WILLIE. Boet Sam! You promised. *(He returns to his work.)*

SAM. Okay, okay! Sorry, Willie.

(HALLY deposits his school case and takes off his raincoat. His clothes are a little neglected and untidy: black blazer with school badge, grey flannel trousers in need of ironing, khaki shirt and tie, black shoes. SAM has fetched a towel for HALLY to dry his hair.)

HALLY. God, what a lousy day. It's coming down cats and dogs out there. Bad for business, chaps ... *(conspiratorial whisper)* ... but it also means we're in for a nice quiet afternoon.

SAM. You can speak loud. Your mom's not here.

HALLY. Out shopping?

SAM. No. The hospital.

HALLY. But it's Thursday. There's no visiting on Thursday afternoons. Is my Dad okay?

SAM. Sounds like it. In fact I think he's going home.

HALLY. *(Stopped short by SAM'S remark.)* What do you mean?

SAM. The hospital phoned.

HALLY. To say what?

SAM. I don't know. I just heard your mom talking.

HALLY. So what makes you say he's going home?

SAM. It sounded as if they were telling her to come and fetch him.

HALLY. *(Thinks about what SAM has said for a few seconds.)* When did she leave?

SAM. About an hour ago. She said she would phone you. Want to eat?

(HALLY doesn't respond.)

SAM. Hally, want your lunch?

HALLY. I suppose so. *(His mood has changed.)* What's on the menu ... as if I don't know.

SAM. Soup, followed by meat pie and gravy.

HALLY. Today's?

SAM. No.

HALLY. And the soup?

SAM. Nourishing pea soup.

HALLY. Just the soup. *(indicating the pile of comic books on the table)* And these?

SAM. For your dad. Mr. Kempston brought them.

HALLY. You haven't been reading them, have you?

SAM. Just looking.

HALLY. *(Leafs through comic books.)* God *what rubbish!* Mental pollution. Take them away.

(SAM exits, waltzing into the kitchen.)

HALLY. *(Turns to WILLIE.)* Did you hear my mom talking on the telephone, Willie?

WILLIE. No, Master Hally. I was at the back.

HALLY. And she didn't say anything to you before she left?

WILLIE. She said I must clean the floors.

HALLY. I mean about Dad.

WILLIE. She don't talk to me about him, Master Hally.

HALLY. *(with conviction)* No! It can't be. They said he needed at least another three weeks of treatment. Sam's definitely made a mistake. *(Rummages through his school case, finds a book and settles down at the table to read.)* So, Willie!

WILLIE. Yes, Master Hally!

HALLY. Grow up, Willie.

WILLIE. Schooling okay today?

HALLY. Yes, okay ...... *(He thinks about it.)* ... no, not really. Ah, what's the difference? I don't care. And Sam says you've got problems.

WILLIE. Big problems.

HALLY. Which leg is sore?

(WILLIE groans.)

HALLY. Both legs?

WILLIE. There is nothing wrong with my legs. Sam is just making jokes.

HALLY. So then you *will* be in the competition.

WILLIE. Only if I can find me a partner.

HALLY. But what about Hilda?

SAM. *(returning with a bowl of soup)* She's the one who's got trouble with her legs.

HALLY. What sort of trouble, Willie?

SAM. From the way he describes it, I think the lady has gone a bit lame.

HALLY. Good God! Have you taken her to see a doctor?

SAM. I think a vet would be better.

HALLY. What do you mean?

SAM. What do you call it again, when a racehorse goes very fast?

HALLY. Gallop?

SAM. That's it!

WILLIE. Boet Sam!

HALLY. "A gallop down the home-stretch to the winning post." But what's that got to do with Hilda?

SAM. Count Basie always gets there first.

(WILLIE lets fly with his slop-rag. It misses SAM and hits HALLY.)

HALLY. *(furious)* For Christ's sake, Willie! What the hell do you think you're doing!

WILLIE. Sorry Master Hally, but it's him....

HALLY. Act your bloody age! *(Hurls the rag back at WILLIE.)* Cut out the nonsense now and get on with your work. And you too, Sam. Stop fooling around.

(SAM moves away.)

HALLY. No, hang on — I haven't finished! Tell me exactly what my mom said.

SAM. I have. "When Hally comes, tell him I've gone to the hospital and I'll phone him."

HALLY. She didn't say anything about taking my dad home?

SAM. No. It's just that, when she was talking on the phone...

HALLY. *(interrupting him)* No, Sam. They can't be discharging him. She would have said so if they were. In any case, we saw him last night and he wasn't in good shape at all. Staff-nurse even said there was talk about taking x-rays. And now suddenly today he's better? If anything, it sounds more like a bad turn to me ... which I sincerely hope it isn't. Hang on ... how long ago did you say she left?

SAM. Just before two ... *(Checks his wristwatch.)* ... hour and a half.

HALLY. I know how to settle it. *(Goes behind the counter to the telephone, talking as he dials.)* Let's give her ten minutes to get to the hospital, ten minutes to load him up, another ten, at the most, to get home and another ten to get him inside. Forty minutes. They should have been home for at least half an hour already. *(Pause. He waits with the receiver to his ear.)* No reply. And you know why? Because she's at his bedside in the hospital, helping him pull through a bad turn. You definitely heard wrong.

SAM. Okay.

(As far as HALLY is concerned, the matter is settled. He returns to his table, sits down and divides his attention between the book and his soup.)

SAM. *(He is at the school case and picks up a text-book.)* "Modern Graded Mathematics for Standards Nine and Ten." *(Opens it at random and laughs at something he sees.)* Who is this supposed to be?

HALLY. Old fart-face Prentice.

SAM. Teacher?

HALLY. Thinks he is. And believe me, that is not a bad likeness.

SAM. Has he seen it?

HALLY. Yes.

SAM. What did he say?

HALLY. Tried to be clever as usual. Said I was no Leonardo Da Vinci and that bad art had to be punished. So, six of the best, and his are bloody good.

SAM. On the bum?

HALLY. Where else? The days when I got them on my hands are gone forever, Sam.

SAM. With your trousers down?

HALLY. No. He's not quite that barbaric.

SAM. That's the way they do it in gaol.

HALLY. *(flicker of morbid interest)* Really?

SAM. Ja. When the magistrate sentences "strokes with a light cane".

HALLY. Go on.

SAM. They make you lie down on a bench. One policeman pulls your shirt over your head and holds your arms, another one pulls down your trousers and holds your ankles...

HALLY. Thank you! That's enough.

SAM. ... and the one that gives you the strokes talks to you gently and for a long time between each one. *(He laughs.)*

HALLY. I've heard enough *Sam*! Jesus! It's a bloody awful world when you come to think of it. People can be real bastards.

[handwritten margin note: He used 'you', not 'I']

SAM. That's the way it is, Hally.

HALLY. It doesn't *have* to be that way. There is something called progress, you know. We don't exactly burn people at the stake anymore.

[handwritten margin note: He doesn't really take care(ful) consideration with his words]

SAM. Like Joan of Arc.

HALLY. Correct. If she was captured today she'd be given a fair trial.

SAM. And then the death sentence.

HALLY. *(a world-weary sigh)* I know, I know! I os*k*illate *(mispronounces)* between hope and despair for this world as well, Sam. But things will change, you wait and see. One day somebody is going to get up and give history a kick up the backside and get it going again.

SAM. Like who?

HALLY. *(after thought)* They're called Social Reformers. Every age, Sam, has got its Social Reformer. My history book is full of them.

SAM. So where's ours? *[handwritten: (Great question!)]*

HALLY. Good question. And I hate to say it but the answer is: I don't know. Maybe he hasn't even been born yet. Or is still only a babe in arms at his mother's breast. God, what a thought.

SAM. So we just go on waiting.

HALLY. Ja, looks like it. *(back to his soup and book)*

[handwritten note with arrow: mocking or what?]

I will marry when I want (penis reference comes to mind)

SAM. *(reading from the textbook)* "Introduction: In some mathematical problems only the magnitude...." (He mispronounces the word, "magnitude.")

HALLY. *(correcting him without looking up)* Magnitude.

SAM. What's it mean?

HALLY. How big it is. The size of the thing.

SAM. *(reading)* "... magnitude of the quantities is of importance. In other problems we need to know whether these quantities are negative or positive. For example, whether there is a debit or credit bank balance...."

HALLY. Whether you're broke or not.

SAM. "... whether the temperature is above or below zero ...."

HALLY. Nought degrees. Cheerful state of affairs! No cash and you're freezing to death. Mathematics won't get you out of that one.

SAM. "All these quantities are called...." *(spelling the word)* "... s - c - a - l ..."

HALLY. Scalers.

SAM. Scalers! *(shaking his head with a laugh)* You understand all that?

HALLY. *(turning a page)* No. And I don't intend to try.

SAM. So what happens when the exams come?

HALLY. Failing a maths exam isn't the end of the world, Sam. How many times have I told you that examination results don't measure intelligence?

SAM. I would say about as many times as you've failed one of them.

HALLY. *(mirthlessly)* Ha, ha, ha. Just remember, Winston Churchill didn't do particularly well at school.

SAM. You've also told me that one many times.

HALLY. Well it just so happens to be the truth.

SAM. Mag-ni-tude, show me how to use it.

HALLY. *(after thought)* An intrepid social reformer will not be daunted by the magnitude of the task he has undertaken.

SAM. *(impressed)* Couple of jaw-breakers in there!

HALLY. I gave you three for the price of one. Intrepid, daunted and magnitude. I did that once in an exam. Put five of the words I had to explain in one sentence. It was half a page long.

SAM. Well, I'll put my money on you in the English exam.

HALLY. Piece of cake. Eighty percent without even trying.

SAM. *(another textbook from HALLY'S case)* And history?

HALLY. So so. I'll scrape through. In the fifties, if I'm lucky.

SAM. You didn't do *too* badly last year.

HALLY. Because we had World War One. That at least had some action. You try to find that in the South African Parliamentary system.

SAM. *(reading from the history textbook)* "Napoleon and the principle of equality." Hey! This sounds interesting. "After concluding peace with Britain in 1802, Napoleon used a brief period of calm to in-sti-tute..."

HALLY. Introduce.

SAM. "... many reforms. Napoleon regarded all people as equal before the law and wanted them to have equal opportunities for advancement. All ves-ti-ges of the feudal system with its oppression of the poor were abolished." Vestiges, feudal system and abolished. I'm alright on oppression.

HALLY. I'm thinking. He swept away — abolished — the last remains — vestiges — of the bad old days — feudal system.

SAM. Ha! There's the social reformer we're waiting for. He sounds like a man of some magnitude.

HALLY. I'm not so sure about that. It's a damn good title for a book though. A man of magnitude!

SAM. He sounds pretty big to me, Hally.

HALLY. Don't confuse historical significance with greatness. But maybe I'm being a bit prejudiced. Have a look in there and you'll see he's two chapters long. And hell! ... has he only got dates, Sam, all of which you've got to remember! This campaign and that campaign, and then because of all the fighting the next thing is we get peace treaties all over the place. And what's the end of the story? Battle of Waterloo, which he looses. Wasn't worth it. No, I don't know about him as a man of magnitude.

Favors war over peace

SAM. Then who would you say was?

HALLY. To answer that we need a definition of greatness, and I suppose that would be somebody who .... somebody who benefited all mankind.

SAM. Right. But like who?

HALLY. *(He speaks with total conviction.)* Charles Darwin. Remember *him*? That big book from the library. *The Origin of the Species.*

SAM. Him?

HALLY. Yes. For his Theory of Evolution.

SAM. *You* didn't finish it.

HALLY. I ran out of time. I didn't finish it because my two weeks was up. But I'm going to take it out again after

I've digested what I read. It's safe. I've hidden it away in the theology section. Nobody ever goes in there. And anyway, who are you to talk? You hardly even looked at it.

SAM. I tried. I looked at the chapters in the beginning and I saw one called "The struggle for an existence." Ah ha, I thought. At last! But what did I get? Something called the mistiltoe which needs the apple tree and there's too many seeds and all are going to die except for one.......! No, Hally.

HALLY. *(intellectually outraged)* What do you mean, *no!* The poor man had to start somewhere. For God's sake, Sam, he revolutionised science. Now we know.

SAM. What? *(He picks up soup bowl.)*

HALLY. Where we came from and what it all means.

SAM. And that's a benefit to mankind? *Anyway,* I still don't believe it. *(He goes behind bar.)*

HALLY. God, you're impossible. I showed it to you in black and white.

SAM. Doesn't mean I got to believe it.

HALLY. It's the likes of you that kept the inquisition in business. It's called bigotry. Anyway, that's my man of magnitude. Mr. Charles Darwin! Who's yours?

SAM. *(without hesitation)* Mr. Abraham Lincoln.

HALLY. I might have guessed as much. Don't get sentimental, Sam. You've never been a slave, you know. And anyway, we freed your ancestors here in South Africa long before the Americans. But if you want to thank somebody on their behalf, do it to Mr. William Wilberforce. Come on. Try again. I want a real genius. *(Now enjoying himself, he goes behind the counter and helps himself to a chocolate.)*

SAM. *(also enjoying himself)* Mr. William Shakespeare.

[handwritten margin notes:] Finally getting somewhere

[handwritten note at bottom:] This boy does not have respect for people's views but his own whole hearted

HALLY. *(no enthusiasm)* Oh. So you're also one of them, are you. You're basing that opinion on only one play, you know. You've only read my *Julius Caesar* and even I don't understand half of what they're talking about. They should do what they did with the old Bible: bring the language up to date.

SAM. That's all you've got. It's also the only one *you've* read.

HALLY. I know. I admit it. That's why I suggest we reserve our judgement until we've checked up on a few others. I've got a feeling, though, that by the end of this year, one is going to be enough for me, and I can give you the names of twenty-nine other chaps in the standard nine class of the Port Elizabeth Technical College who feel the same. But if you want him you can have him. My turn now. *(pacing)* This is a damned good exercise, you know! It started off looking like a simple question and here it's got us really probing into the intellectual heritage of our civilization.

small minded

SAM. So who is it going to be?

HALLY. My next man ... and he gets the title on two scores: social reform and literary genius ... is Leo Nikolaevich *(mispronounces)* Tolstoy.

SAM. That Russian.

HALLY. Correct. Remember the picture of him I showed you?

SAM. With the long beard.

HALLY. *(trying to look like Tolstoy)* And those burning, visionary eyes. My God, the face of a social prophet if ever I saw one! And remember my words when I showed it to you? Here's a *man*, Sam!

a romance *

SAM. Those were words, Hally.

HALLY. Not many intellectuals are prepared to shovel manure with the peasants and then go home and write a "little book" called *War and Peace.* Incidentally, Sam, he was somebody else who, to quote ... "did not distinguish himself, scholastically."

SAM. Meaning?

HALLY. He was also no good at school.

SAM. Like you and Winston Churchill. Ha, ha, ha.

HALLY. Don't get clever, Sam. That man freed his serfs of his own free will.

SAM. No argument. He was a somebody alright. I accept him.

HALLY. I'm sure Count Tolstoy will be very pleased to hear that. Your turn. Shoot. *(Has another chocolate from behind the counter.)* I'm waiting, Sam.

SAM. I've got him.

HALLY. Good. Submit your candidate for examination.

SAM. Jesus.

HALLY. *(stopped dead in his tracks)* Who?

SAM. Jesus Christ.

HALLY. Oh come on, Sam!

SAM. The messiah.

HALLY. Ja, but still.... No, Sam. Don't let's get started on religion. We'll just spend the whole afternoon arguing again. Suppose I turn around and say Mohammed?

SAM. Alright.

HALLY. You can't have them both on the same list!

SAM. Why not? You like Mohammed, I like Jesus.

HALLY. I *don't* like Mohammed. I never have. I was

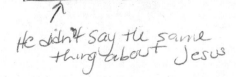

He didn't say the same thing about Jesus

"Suppose"

merely being hypothetical. As far as I'm concerned, the Koran is as bad as the Bible. No. Religion is out! I'm not going to waste my time again, arguing with you about the existence of God. You know perfectly well I'm an athiest and I've got homework to do.

SAM. Okay, I take him back.

HALLY. You've got time for one more name.

SAM. I've got one I know we'll agree on. A simple straight-forward great Man of Magnitude .... and no arguments. And *he* really *did* benefit all mankind.

HALLY. I wonder. After your last contribution, I'm beginning to doubt whether anything in the way of an intellectual agreement is possible between the two of us. Who is he?

SAM. Guess.

HALLY. Socrates?

SAM. No. *(Shakes his head.)*

HALLY. Alexandre Dumas?

SAM. No. *(Shakes his head.)*

HALLY. Karl Marx?

SAM. No. *(Shakes his head.)*

HALLY. Dostoevsky?

SAM. No. *(Shakes his head.)*

HALLY. Nietzsche?

SAM. No. *(Shakes his head.)*

HALLY. Give me a clue.

SAM. The letter "P" is important...

HALLY. Plato!

SAM. ...and his name begins with an "F."

HALLY. I got it. Freud and psychology.

SAM. No. I didn't understand him.

HALLY. That makes two of us.

SAM. Think of mouldy apricot jam.

HALLY. *(after a delighted laugh)* Penicillim and Sir Alexander Flemming! And the title of the book: *The Microbe Hunters. (delighted)* Splendid, Sam! Splendid. For once we are in total agreement. The major breakthrough in medical science in the 20th century. If it wasn't for him, we might have lost the Second World War. It's deeply gratifying, Sam, to know that I haven't been wasting my time in talking to you. *(strutting around proudly)* Tolstoy may have educated his peasants, but I've educated you.

SAM. Standard four to standard nine.

HALLY. Have we been at it as long as that?

SAM. Yep. And my first lesson was geography.

HALLY. *(intrigued)* Really? I don't remember.

SAM. My room there at the back of the old Jubilee Boarding House. I had just started working for your Mom. Little boy in short trousers walks in one afternoon and asks me, seriously: Sam, do you want to see South Africa? Hey man! Sure I wanted to see South Africa!

HALLY. Was that me?

SAM. So the next thing I'm looking at a map you had just done for homework. It was your first one and you were very proud of yourself.

HALLY. Go on.

SAM. Then came my first lesson. "Repeat after me, Sam: gold in the Transvaal, mealies in the Free State, sugar in Natal and grapes in the Cape." I still know it!

HALLY. Well I'll be buggered. So that's how it all started.

SAM. And your next map was one with all the rivers and

the mountains they came from. The Orange, the Vaal, the Limpopo, the Zambesi...

HALLY. You've got a phenomenal memory.

SAM. You should be grateful. That is why you started passing your exams. You tried to be better than me.

Interesting to know

(They laugh together. WILLIE is attracted by the laughter and joins them.)

HALLY. The old Jubilee Boarding House. Sixteen rooms with board and lodging, rent in advance and one week's notice. I haven't thought about it for donkey's years ... and I don't think that's an accident. God, was I glad when we sold it and moved out. Those years are not remembered as the happiest ones of an unhappy childhood.

WILLIE. *(knocking on the table and trying to imitate a woman's voice)* "Hally, are you there?"

HALLY. Who's that supposed to be?

WILLIE. "What you doing in there, Hally? Come out at once!"

HALLY. *(to SAM)* What's he talking about?

SAM. Don't you remember?

WILLIE. "Sam, Willie ... is he in there with you boys?"

SAM. Hiding away in our room when your mother was looking for you.

HALLY. *(another good laugh)* Of course! I use to crawl and hide under your bed! But finish the story, Willie. Then what used to happen? You chaps would give the game away by telling her I was in there with you. So much for friendship.

SAM. We couldn't lie to her. She knew.

HALLY. Which meant I got another rowing for hanging around the "servant's quarters". I think I spent more time in there with you chaps than anywhere else in that dump. And do you blame me? Nothing but bloody misery wherever you went. Somebody was always complaining about the food or my mother was having a fight with Micky Nash because she'd caught her with a petty officer in her room. Maud Meiring was another one. Remember those two? They were prostitutes, you know. Soldiers and sailors from the troopships. Bottom fell out of the business when the war ended. God, the flotsam and jetsam that life washed up on our shores! No joking, if it wasn't for your room I would have been the first certified ten-year-old in medical history. Ja, the memories are coming back now. Walking home from school and thinking: What can I do this afternoon? Try out a few ideas but sooner or later I'd end up in there with you fellows. I bet you I could still find my way to your room with my eyes closed. *(He does exactly that.)* Down the corridor ... telephone on the right which my mom keeps locked because somebody is using it on the sly and not paying ... past the kitchen and unappetising cooking smells ... around the corner into the backyard, hold my breath again because there are more smells coming when I pass your lavatory, then into that little passageway, first door on the right and into your room. How's that?

SAM. Good. But as usual, you forgot to knock.

HALLY. Like that time I barged in and caught you and ... Cynthia at it — remember? God, was I embarassed! I didn't know what was going on at first.

Invaded by a little boy wav

SAM. Ja, that taught you a lesson.

HALLY. And about a lot more than knocking on doors, I'll have you know, and I don't mean geography either. Hell Sam, couldn't you have waited until it was dark?

SAM. No.

HALLY. Was it that urgent?

SAM. Yes, and if you don't believe me, wait until your time comes.

HALLY. No thank you. I am not interested in girls. *(Back to his memories ... he stands in the middle of the same room, pointing as he lists the items.)* A cold little room with a grey cement floor. Your bed against that wall ... and I now know why the mattress sags so much! ... Willie's bed ... it's propped up on bricks because one leg is broken ... that wobbly little table with the wash-basin and jug of water ... Yes! ... Stuck to the wall above it are some pin-up pictures from magazines. Joe Louis ...

WILLIE. Brown Bomber. World Title. *(boxing pose)* Three rounds and knock-out.

HALLY. Against who?

SAM. Max Schmelling.

HALLY. Correct. I can also remember Fred Astaire and Ginger Rogers and Rita Hayworth in a bathing costume which always made me hot and bothered when I looked at it. Under Willie's bed is an old suitcase with all his clothes in a mess which is why I never hide there. Your things are neat and tidy in a trunk next to your bed, and on it there is a picture of you and Cynthia in your ballroom clothes, your first silver cup for third-place in a competition and an old radio which doesn't work anymore. Have I left out anything?

SAM. No.

HALLY. Right, so much for stage-directions. Now the characters. Willie is in bed, under his blankets with his clothes on, complaining non-stop about something, but we can't make out a word of what he's saying because he's got his head under the blankets, as well. You're on your bed trimming your toenails with a knife — not a very edifying sight — and as for me.... What am I doing?

SAM. You're sitting on the floor, giving Willie a lecture about being a good loser while you get the checker board and pieces ready for a game. Then you go to Willie's bed, pull off the blankets and make him play with you first because you know you're going to win, and that gives you the second game with me.

HALLY. And you certainly were a bad loser, Willie!

WILLIE. Haai!

HALLY. Wasn't he, Sam? And so slow! A game with you almost took the whole afternoon. Thank God I gave up trying to teach you how to play chess.

WILLIE. You and Sam cheated.

HALLY. I never saw Sam cheat, and mine were mostly the mistakes of youth.

WILLIE. Then how is it you two was always winning?

HALLY. Have you ever considered the possibility, Willie, that it is because we were better than you?

WILLIE. Everytime better?

HALLY. Not every time. There were occasions when we deliberately let you win a game so that you would stop sulking and go on playing with us. Sam used to wink at me when you weren't looking to show me it was time to let you win.

WILLIE. So then you two didn't play fair.

HALLY. It was for your benefit Mr. Malopo, which is more than being fair. It was an act of self-sacrifice. *(to SAM)* But you know what my best memory is, don't you?

SAM. No.

HALLY. Come on, guess. If your memory is so good, you must remember it as well.

SAM. We got up to a lot of tricks in there, Hally.

HALLY. This one was special, Sam.

SAM. I'm listening.

HALLY. It started off looking like another of those use-less, nothing-to-do afternoons. I'd already been down to Main Street looking for adventure, but nothing had happened. I didn't feel like climbing trees in the Donkin park, or pretending I was a private eye and following a stranger ... so, as usual: See what's cooking in Sam's room. This time it was you on the floor. You had two thin pieces of wood and you were smoothing them down with a knife. It didn't look particularly interesting, but when I asked you what you were doing, you just said, "Wait and see, Hally. Wait ... and see." ... in that secret sort of way of yours, so I knew there was a surprise coming. You teased me, you bugger, by being deliberately slow and not answering my questions!

(SAM laughs.)

HALLY. And whistling while you worked away! God, it was infuriating! I could have brained you! It was only when you tied them together in a cross and put that down on the brown paper that I realized what you were doing. Sam is making a kite! And when I asked you, you said: Yes.......! *(shaking his head with disbelief)* The sheer audacity of it took my breath away. I mean seriously, what the hell does a black man know about flying a kite? I'll be honest with you, Sam, I had no hopes for it. If you think I was excited and happy, you got another guess coming. In fact I was shit-scared that we were going to make fools of ourselves. When we left the boarding house to go up onto the hill, I was praying quietly that there wouldn't be any other kids around to laugh at us.

SAM. *(enjoying the memory as much as HALLY)* Ja, I could see that.

HALLY. I made it obvious, did I?

SAM. Ja. He refused to carry it.

HALLY. Do you blame me? Can you remember what the poor thing looked like? Tomato-box wood and brown paper! Flour and water for glue! Two of my mother's old stockings for a tail and then all those bits and pieces of string you made me tie together so that we could fly it! Hell no, that was now only asking for a miracle to happen.

SAM. Then the big argument when I told you to hold the string and run with it when I let go.

HALLY. I was prepared to run alright, but straight back to the boarding house.

SAM. *(knowing what's coming)* So what happened?

HALLY. Come on Sam, you remember as well as I do.

SAM. I want to hear it from you.

HALLY. *(Pauses; wants to be as accurate as possible.)* You went a little distance from me down the hill, you held it up ready to let it go ... This is it I thought. Like everything else in my life, here comes another fiasco. Then you shouted, "Go Hally!" and I started to run. *(another pause)* I don't know how to describe it, Sam. Ja! The miracle happened! I was running, waiting for it to crash to the ground, but instead suddenly there was something alive behind me at the end of the string, tugging at it as if it wanted to be free. I looked back.... *(Shakes his head.)* ... I still can't believe my eyes. It was flying! Looping around and trying to climb even higher into the sky. You shouted to me to let it have more string. I did, until there was none left, and I was just holding that piece of wood we had tied it to. You came up and joined me. You were laughing.

SAM. So were you. And shouting, "It works, Sam! We've done it!"

HALLY. And we had! I was so proud of us! It was the most splendid thing I had ever seen. I wished there were hundreds of kids around to watch us. The part that scared me though, was when you showed me how to make it dive down to the ground and then swoop up again, just when it was on the point of crashing.

SAM. He didn't want to try, himself.

HALLY. Of course not! I would have been suicidal if anything had happened to it. Watching you do it made me nervous enough. I was quite happy just to see it up there with its tail fluttering behind it. You left me after that, didn't you? You explained how to get it down, we tied it to the bench so that I could sit and watch it, and you went away. I wanted you to stay, you know. I was a little scared of having to look after it by myself.

SAM. *(quietly)* I had work to do, Hally.

HALLY. It was sort of sad bringing it down, Sam. And it looked sad again when it was lying there on the ground. Like something that had lost its soul. Just tomato-box wood, brown paper and two of my mother's old stockings! But hell, I'll never forget that first moment when I saw it up there. I had a stiff neck the next day from looking up so much.

(SAM laughs.)

HALLY. *(Turns to him with a question he never thought of asking before.)* Why did you make me that kite, Sam?

SAM. *(evenly)* I can't remember.

HALLY. Truly?

SAM. Too long ago, Hally.

HALLY. Ja, I suppose it was. It's time for another one, you know.

SAM. Why do you say that?

HALLY. Because it feels like that. Wouldn't be a good day to fly it though.

SAM. No. You can't fly kites on rainy days.

HALLY. *(He studies SAM. Their memories have made him conscious of the man's presence in his life.)* How old are you, Sam?

SAM. Two score and ten.

HALLY. Strange, isn't it?

SAM. What?

HALLY. Me and you.

SAM. What's strange about it?

HALLY. Little white boy in short trousers and a black man, old enough to be his father, flying a kite. It's not every day you see that.

SAM. But why strange? Because the one is white and the other black?

HALLY. I don't know. Would have been just as strange I suppose if it had been me and my dad ... cripple man and a little boy! Nope! There's no chance of me flying a kite without it being strange. *(simple statement of fact—no self-pity)* There's a nice little short-story there. "The Kite-Flyers" But we'd have to find a twist in the ending.

SAM. Twist?

HALLY. Yes. Something unexpected. The way it ended with us was too straight-forward .... me on the bench and you going back to work. There's no drama in that.

WILLIE. And me?

HALLY. You want to get into the story as well, do you? — I got it! — Change the title: "Afternoons in Sam's Room" ... expand it and tell all the stories. It's on its way to being a novel. Our days in the old Jubilee. Sad in a way, that they're over. I almost wish we were still in that little room.

SAM. We're still together.

HALLY. That's true. It's just that life felt the right size in there ... not too big and not too small. Wasn't so hard to work up a bit of courage. It's got so bloody complicated since then.

(The telephone rings. SAM answers it.)

SAM. *(into phone)* St. Georges Park Tea Room ... Hello Madam ... Yes Madam, he's here ... *(to HALLY)* Hally, it's your mother.

HALLY. Where is she phoning from?

SAM. Sounds like the hospital. It's a public telephone.

HALLY. *(relieved)* You see! I told you. *(into the telephone)* Hello Mom ... Yes ... Yes no fine. Everything's under control here. How's things with poor old Dad? Has he had a bad turn? ... What? ... Oh God! ... Yes, Sam told me but I was sure he'd made a mistake. But what's this all about, Mom? He didn't look at all good last night. How can he get better so quickly? ... Then very obviously you must say no. Be firm with him. You're the boss. You know what it's going to be like if he comes home.... Well then don't blame me when I fail my exams at the end of the year.... Yes! How am I expected to be fresh for school when I spend half the night massaging his gammy leg.... So am I! ... So tell him a white lie. Say Dr. Colley wants more x-rays of his stump. Or bribe him. We'll sneak in double tots of brandy in future.... What? ... Order him to get back into bed at once! If he's going to behave like a child, treat him like one.... Alright, Mom! I was just trying to... I'm sorry.... I said I'm sorry.... Quick, give me your number. I'll phone you back. *(He hangs-up and waits a few seconds.)* Here we go again. *(He dials.)* I'm sorry, Mom.... Okay.... But now listen to me carefully. All it needs is for you to put your foot down. Don't take no for an answer.... Did you hear me? And whatever you do, don't discuss it with him.... Because I'm frightened you'll give in to him.... Yes, Sam gave me lunch.... I ate all of it! ... No, Mom, not a soul. It's still raining here.... Right, I'll tell them. I'll just do some homework and then lock-up.... But remember no, Mom. Don't listen to anything he says. And phone me

back and let me know what happens.... Okay. Bye Mom.
(He hangs up.)

This is the best Justification he has

(The men are staring at him.)

HALLY. My mom says that, when you're finished with
the floors you must do the windows. *(pause)* Don't misun-
derstand me, chaps. All I want is for him to get better. And
if he was, I'd be the first person to say: Bring him home.
But he's not and we can't give him the medical care and
attention he needs at home. That's what hospitals are
there for. *(brusquely)* So don't just stand there! Get on
with it!

(SAM clears HALLY'S table.)

HALLY. You heard right. My Dad wants to go home.
SAM. Is he better?
HALLY. *(sharply)* No! How the hell can he be better
when last night he was groaning with pain. This is not an
age of miracles!
SAM. Then he should stay in hospital.
HALLY. *(seething with irritation and frustration)* Tell me
something I don't know, Sam. What the hell do you think
I was saying to my mom. All I can say is fuck-it-all.
SAM. I'm sure he'll listen to your mom.
HALLY. *(trying to hide his true feelings)* You don't know
what she's up against. He's already packed his shaving-kit
and pyjamas and is sitting on his bed with his crutches,
dressed and ready to go. I know him when he gets in that
mood. If she tries to reason with him, we've had it. She's

no match for him when it comes to a batle of words. He'll tie her in knots.

SAM. I suppose it gets lonely for him in there.

HALLY. With all the patients and nurses around? Regular visits from the Salvation Army? Balls! It's ten times worse for him at home. I'm at school and my mother is here in the business all day.

SAM. He's at least got you at night.

HALLY. *(before he can stop himself)* And we've got him! *(another cover)* Please! I don't want to talk about it anymore. *(Unpacks his schoolcase, slamming down books on the table.)* Life is just a plain bloody mess, that's all. And people are fools.

SAM. Come on, Hally.

HALLY. Yes they are! They bloody-well deserve what they get.

SAM. Then don't complain.

HALLY. Don't try to be clever, Sam. It doesn't suit you. Anybody who thinks there's nothing wrong with this world needs to have his head examined. Just when things are going along all right, without fail someone or something will come along and spoil everything. Somebody should write that down as a fundamental law of the universe. The principle of perpetual disappointment. If there is a God who created this world, he should scrap it and try again.

SAM. Alright, Hally, alright. What you got for homework?

HALLY. Bullshit, as usual. *(Opens an exercise book and reads.)* "Write five-hundred words describing an annual event of cultural or historical significance."

What a Beat

SAM. That should be easy enough for you.

HALLY. And also plain bloody boring. You know what he wants, don't you? One of their useless, old ceremonies. The commemoration of the landing of the eighteen-twenty settlers, or, if it's going to be culture, Carols By Candlelight every Christmas.

SAM. It's an impressive sight. Make a good description, Hally. All those candles glowing in the dark and the people singing hymns.

HALLY. And it's called religious hysteria. *(intense irritation)* Please, Sam! Just leave me alone and let me get on with it. I'm not in the mood for games this afternoon. And remember my mom's orders. You're to help Willie with the windows. Come on now, I don't want any more nonsense in here.

SAM. Okay, Hally, okay.

(HALLY settles down to his homework; determined preparations ... pen, ruler, exercise-book, dictionary, another cake ... all of which will lead to nothing. SAM waltzes over to WILLIE and starts to replace tbles and chairs. He practices a ballroom step while doing so. WILLIE watches, and when SAM is finished, he gets up and tries.)

SAM. Good! But just a little bit quicker on the turn and only move into her after she's crossed over. What about this one? *(another step.)*

(When SAM is finished, WILLIE again has a go.)

SAM. Much better. See what happens when you just

relax, and enjoy yourself. Remember that in two weeks time and you'll be alright.

WILLIE. But I haven't got partner, Boet Sam.

SAM. Maybe Hilda will turn up tonight.

WILLIE. *(He has no hope of that.)* No, Boet Sam. *(reluctantly)* I gave her a good hiding.

SAM. You mean a bad one.

WILLIE. Good bad one.

SAM. Then you mustn't complain either. Now you pay the price for losing your temper.

WILLIE. I also pay two pounds ten shilling entrance fee.

SAM. They'll refund you if you withdraw now.

WILLIE. *(appalled)* You mean don't dance?

SAM. Yes.

WILLIE. No! I wait too long and I practise too hard. If I find me new partner, you think I can be ready in two weeks? I ask madam for leave now and we practise every day.

SAM. Quickstep, non-stop for two week. World record, Willie, but you'll be mad at the end.

WILLIE. No jokes, Boet Sam.

SAM. I'm not joking.

WILLIE. So then what?

SAM. Find Hilda. Say you're sorry and promise you won't beat her again.

WILLIE. No.

SAM. Then withdraw. Try again next year.

WILLIE. No.

SAM. Then I give up.

WILLIE. Haaikona, Boet Sam, you can't.

SAM. What do you mean, I can't. I'm telling you: I give up.

WILLIE. *(adamant)* No! *(accusingly)* It was you who start me ballroom dancing.

SAM. So?

WILLIE. Before that I use to be happy. And is you and Miriam who bring me to Hilda and say, "Here's partner for you."

SAM. What are you saying, Willie?

WILLIE. You!

SAM. But me what? To blame?

WILLIE. Yes.

SAM. Willie....? *(Bursts into laughter.)*

WILLIE. And now all you do is make jokes at me. You wait. When Miriam leaves you, is my turn to laugh. Ha, ha, ha.

SAM. *(He can't take WILLIE seriously any longer.)* She can leave me tonight! I know what to do. *(bowing before an imaginary partner)* May I have the pleasure? *(He dances and sings.)*

JUST A FELLOW AND HIS PILLOW
DANCING LIKE A WILLOW,
IN AN AUTUMN BREEZE.

WILLIE. There you go again!

(SAM goes on dancing and singing.)

WILLIE. Boet Sam!

SAM. There's the answer to your problem! Judges announcement in two weeks time: "Ladies and Gentlemen, the winner in the open section ... Mr. Willie Malopo and his pillow.

(This is too much for a now really angry WILLIE. He goes for SAM but the latter is too quick for him and puts HALLY'S table between the two of them.)

HALLY. *(exploding)* For Christ's sake, you two!

WILLIE. *(still trying to get at SAM)* I donner you, Sam! Struesgod!

SAM. *(still laughing)* Sorry, Willie.... Sorry...

HALLY. Sam! Willie! *(Grabs his ruler and gives WILLIE a vicious whack on the bum.)* How the hell am I supposed to concentrate with the two of you behaving like bloody children!

WILLIE. Hit him too!

HALLY. Shut-up, Willie.

WILLIE. He started jokes again.

HALLY. Get back to your work. You too, Sam. *(his ruler.)* Do you want another one, Willie?

(SAM and WILLIE return to their work.)

HALLY. *(Uses the opportunity to escape from his unsuccessful attempt at homework. He struts around like a little Hitler, ruler in hand, giving vent to his anger and frustration.)* Suppose a customer had walked in then; or the Park Superintendent? And seen the two of you behaving like a pair of hooligans. That would have been the end of my mother's license, you know. And your jobs! Well, this is the end of it. From now on there will be no more of your ballroom nonsense in here. This is a business establishment, not a bloody New Brighton dancing school. I've been far too lenient with the two of you. *(Goes behind the counter for a green cooldrink and a dollop of ice-cream. He keeps up his tirade as he prepares it.)* But what really makes me bitter is that I allow you chaps a little freedom in here — when business is bad — and what do you do with it? The foxtrot! 'Specially you, Sam. There's more to life than trotting around a dance floor and I thought at least *you* knew it.

SAM. It's a harmless pleasure, Hally. It doesn't hurt anybody.

HALLY. It's also a rather simple one, you know.

SAM. You reckon so? Have you ever tried?

HALLY. Of course not.

SAM. Why don't you? Now.

HALLY. What do you mean? Me dance?

SAM. Yes. I'll show you a simple step — the waltz — then you try it.

HALLY. What will that prove?

SAM. That it might not be as easy as you think.

HALLY. I didn't say it was easy I said it was simple — like in simple-minded, meaning mentally retarded. You can't exactly say it challenges the intellect.

SAM. It does other things.

HALLY. Such as?

SAM. Make people happy.

HALLY. *(the glass in his hand)* So do American cream sodas with ice-cream. For God's sake, Sam, you're not asking me to take ballroom dancing serious, are you?

SAM. Yes.

HALLY. *(sigh of defeat)* Oh well, so much for trying to give you a decent education. I've obviously achieved nothing.

SAM. You still haven't told me what's wrong with admiring something that's beautiful and then trying to do it yourself.

the man is trying to educate him simply but he can't tell how sad

HALLY. Nothing. But we happen to be talking about a foxtrot, not a thing of beauty.

SAM. But that is just what I'm saying. If you were to see two champions doing it, two masters of the art....!

HALLY. Oh, God, I give up. So now it's also art!

SAM. Ja.

HALLY. There's a limit, Sam. Don't confuse art and entertainment.

SAM. So then what is art?

HALLY. You want a definition?

SAM. Ja.

HALLY. *(He realizes he has got to be careful. He gives the matter a lot of thought before answering.)* Philosophers have been trying to do that for centuries. What is art? What is life? But basically I suppose it's .... the giving of meaning to matter.

SAM. Nothing to do with beautiful?

HALLY. It goes beyond that. It's the giving of form to the formless.

SAM. Ja, well, maybe it's not art then. But I still say it's beautiful.

HALLY. I'm sure the word you mean to use is entertaining.

SAM. *(adamant)* No. Beautiful. And if you want proof, come along to the Centenary Hall in New Brighton in two weeks time.

(The mention of the Centenary Hall draws WILLIE over to them.)

HALLY. What for? I've seen the two of you prancing

around in here often enough.

SAM. *(He laughs.)* This isn't the real thing, Hally. We're just playing around in here.

HALLY. So? I can use my imagination.

SAM. And what do you get?

HALLY. A lot of people dancing around and having a so-called good time.

SAM. That all?

HALLY. Well basically it is that, surely.

SAM. No it isn't. Your imagination hasn't helped you at all. There's a lot more to it than that. We're getting ready for the championships, Hally, not just another dance. There's going to be a lot of people alright, and they're going to have a good time, but they'll only be spectators, sitting around and watching. It's just the competitors out there on the dance floor. Party decorations and fancy lights all around the walls! The ladies in beautiful evening dresses!

HALLY. My mother's got one of those, Sam, and quite frankly, it's an embarrassment every time she wears it.

SAM. *(undeterred)* Your imagination left out the excitement.

(HALLY scoffs.)

SAM. Oh yes. The finalists are not going to be out there just to have a good time. One of those couples will be the 1950 Eastern Province Champions. And your imagination left out the music.

WILLIE. Mr. Elijah Gladman Guzana and his Orchestral Jazzonians.

SAM. The sound of the big band, Hally. Trombone, trumpet, tenor and alto sax. And then finally, your imagination also left out the climax of the evening when the dancing is finished, the judges have stopped whispering among themselves and the Master of Ceremonies collects their score cards and goes onto the stage to announce the winners.

HALLY. Alright. So you make it sound like a bit of a do. It's an occasion. Satisfied?

SAM. *(victory)* So, you admit *that*!

HALLY. Emotionally, yes, intellectually, no.

SAM. Well I don't know what you mean by that, all I'm telling you is that this is going to be *the* event of the year in New Brighton. It's been sold out for two weeks already. There's only standing room left. We've got competitors coming from Kingwilliamstown, East London, Port Alfred.

HALLY. *(Starts pacing thoughtfully.)* Tell me a bit more.

SAM. I thought you weren't interested ... intellectually.

HALLY. *(mysteriously)* I've got my reasons.

SAM. What do you want to know?

HALLY. It takes place every year?

SAM. Yes. But only every third year in New Brighton. It's East London's turn to have the championships next year.

HALLY. Which, I suppose, makes it an even more significant event.

SAM. Ah ha! We're getting somewhere. Our "occasion" is now a "significant event".

HALLY. I wonder.

SAM. What?

HALLY. I wonder if I would get away with it?

SAM. But what?

HALLY. *(Goes to the table and his exercise book.)* "Write five-hundred words describing an annual event of cultural or historical significance." Would I be stretching poetic license a little too far if I called your Ballroom Championships a cultural event?

SAM. You mean...?

HALLY. You think we could get five-hundred words out of it, Sam?

SAM. Victor Sylvester has written a whole book on ballroom dancing.

WILLIE. You going to write about it, Master Hally?

HALLY. Yes, gentlemen, that is precisely what I am considering doing. Old Doc Bromely — he's my English teacher — is going to argue with me, of course. He doesn't like natives. But I'll point out to him that in strict anthropological terms, the culture of a primitive black society includes its dancing and singing. To put my thesis in a nutshell: the war-dance has been replaced by the waltz. But it still amounts to the same thing; the release of primitive emotions through movement. Shall we give it a go?

SAM. I'm ready.

WILLIE. Me also.

HALLY. Ha! This will teach the old bugger a lesson. *(decision taken)* Right. *(as he turns on lights)* Let's get ourselves organized. *(This means another cake on the table. He sits.)* I think you've given me enough general atmosphere, Sam, but to build the tension and suspense, I need facts. *(pencil poised)*

WILLIE. Give him the facts, Boet Sam.

HALLY. What you called the climax ... how many finalists?

SAM. Six couples.

HALLY. *(making notes)* Go on; give me the picture.

SAM. Spectators seated right around the hall.

HALLY. And it's a full-house.

SAM. At one end, on the stage, Gladman and the Orchestral Jazzonians. At the other end is a long table with three judges. The six finalists go onto the dance floor and take up their positions. When they are ready and the spectators have settled down, the Master of Ceremonies goes to the microphone. To start with, he makes some jokes to get the people laughing...

HALLY. Good touch! *(as he writes)* "...creating a relaxed atmosphere which will change to one of tension and drama as the climax is approached."

SAM. *(onto a chair to act out the M.C.)* Ladies and gentlemen, we have come now to the great moment you have all been waiting for this evening.... The finals of the 1950 Eastern Province Open Ballroom Dancing Championships. But first let me introduce the finalists! Mr and Mrs Welcome Tchabalala from Kingwilliamstown...

WILLIE. *(He applauds after every name.)* Is when the people clap their hands and whistle and make a lot of noise, Master Hally.

SAM. Mr. Mulligan Njikelane and Miss Nomlile Nkonyeni of Grahamstown; Mr. and Mrs Norman Nchinga from Port Alfred; Mr. Fats Bokolane and Miss Dina Plaatjies from East London; Mr. Sipho Dugu and Mrs Mable Magada from Peddie; and from New Brighton our very own Mr. Willie Malopo and Miss Hilda Samuels.

WILLIE. *(Can't believe his ears. He abandons his role as spectators and scrambles into position as a finalist.)* Relaxed and ready to romance!

SAM. The applause dies down. When everybody is silent, Gladman lifts up his sax, nods at the Orchestral Jazzonians..., One-two.....

WILLIE. Play the juke-box please, Boet Sam!

SAM. I also only got busfare, Willie.

HALLY. Hold it, everybody. *(Heads for the cash-register behind the counter.)* How much is in the till, Sam?

SAM. Three Shillings. Hally, your mom counted it before she left.

HALLY. *(Hesitates, then returns to the table.)* Sorry, Willie. You know how she carried on the last time I did it. We'll just have to pool our combined imaginations and hope for the best. Back to work. How are the points scored, Sam?

SAM. Maximum of ten points each for individual style, deportment, rhthym and general appearance.

WILLIE. Must I start?

HALLY. Hold it for a second, Willie. And penalities?

SAM. For what?

HALLY. For doing something wrong. — Say you stumble or bump into somebody ... do they take off any points?

SAM. *(aghast)* Hally...!

HALLY. When you're dancing — if you and your partner collide into another couple. *(He can get no further.)*

SAM. *(Has collapsed with laughter. He explains to WILLIE.)*

/ me and Miriam bump into you and Hilda...

(WILLIE joins him in another good laugh.)

SAM. Hally, Hally...!

HALLY. *(perplexed)* Why? What did I say?

SAM. There's no collisions out there, Hally. Nobody
trips or stumbles or bumps into anybody else. That's
what that moment is all about. To be one of those finalists
on that dance floor is like ... like being in a dream about a
world in which accidents don't happen.

HALLY. *(genuinely moved by Sam's image)* Jesus, Sam!
That's beautiful!

WILLIE. *(Can endure waiting no longer.)* I'm starting. *(He
dances while SAM talks.)*

SAM. Of course it is. That's what I've been trying to say
to you all afternoon. And it's beautiful because that is
what we want life to be like. But instead, like you said, Hally, we're bumping into each other all the time. Look at the
three of us this afternoon: I've bumped into Willie, the
two of us have bumped into you, you've bumped into
your mother, she bumping into your dad.... None of us
knows the steps and there's no music playing. And it
doesn't stop with us. The whole world is doing it all the
time. Open a newspaper and what do you read? America
has bumped into Russia, England is bumping into India,
richman bumps into poorman. Those are big collisions,
Hally. They make for a lot of bruises. People get hurt in all
that bumping, and we're sick and tired of it now. It's been
going on for too long. Are we never going to get it right? ...
learn to dance life like champions instead of always being

just a bunch of beginners at it?

HALLY. *(deep and sincere admiration of the man)* You've got a vision, Sam!

SAM. Not just me. What I'm saying to you is that everybody's got it. That's why there's only standing-room left for the Centenary Hall in two weeks time. For as long as the music lasts we are going to see six couples get it right, the way we want life to be.

HALLY. But is that the best we can do, Sam ... watch six finalists dreaming about the way it should be?

SAM. I don't know. But it starts with that. Without the dream we won't know what we're going for. And anyway, I reckon there are a few people who have got past just dreaming about it and are trying for something real. Remember that thing we read once in the paper about the Mahatma Ghandi? Going without food to stop those riots in India?

HALLY. You're right. He certainly was trying to teach people to get the steps right.

SAM. And the pope.

HALLY. Yes, he's another one. Our old General Smuts as well, you know. He's also out there dancing. You know, Sam, when you come to think of it, that's what the United Nations boils down to ... a dancing school for politicians!

SAM. And let's hope they learn.

HALLY. *(a little surge of hope)* You're right. We mustn't despair. Maybe there's some hope for mankind after all. Keep it up, Willie. *(back to his table with determination)* This is a lot bigger than I thought. So what have we got? Yes, our title: "A World Without Collisions."

SAM. That sounds good! A world without collisions.

HALLY. Sub-title: Global politics on the dance floor. No. A bit too heavy, hey. What about: Ballroom dancing as a political vision. *(As he lowers head to write:)*

(The telephone rings. SAM goes to answer it.)

SAM. St. Georges Park Tea Room.... Yes Madam... Hally, it's your mom.

HALLY. *(back to reality)* O God yes! I'd forgotten all about that. Shit! Remember my words, Sam? Just when you're enjoying yourself, someone or something will come along and wreck everything.

SAM. You haven't heard what she's got to say yet.

HALLY. Public telephone?

SAM. No.

HALLY. Does she sound happy or unhappy?

SAM. I couldn't tell. *(pause)* She's waiting, Hally.

HALLY. (to the telephone) Hello, Mom... No, everything is okay here. Just doing my homework... What's your news?... You've what?... *(Pause. He takes the receiver away from his ear for a few seconds, then goes back to it.)* Yes, I'm still here. Oh well, I give up now. Why did you do it, Mom? ... Well I just hope you know what you've let us in for.... *(loudly)* I said I hope you know what you've let us in for! It's the end of the peace and qiuiet we've been having. *(softly)* Where is he? *(normal voice)* He can't hear us from in there. But for God's sake, Mom, what happened? I told you to be firm with him.... Then you and the nurses should have held him down, taken his crutches away.... I know only too well he's my father! ... I'm not being disrespectful but I'm sick and tired of emptying stinking chamber pots full of plegm and piss ... Yes I do! When you're not there he asks me to do it.... If you really want to know the truth, that's why I've got no appetite for my food.... Yes! There's a lot of things you don't know about. For your information, I still haven't got that science textbook I need. And you know why? He borrowed the money you gave me for it.... Because I didn't want to start another fight between you two.... He says that every-time.... Alright, Mom! *(viciously)* Then just remember to start hiding your bag away again because he'll be at your purse before long for money for booze. And when he's well enough to come down here, you better keep an eye on the till as well, because that is also going to develop a leak.... Then don't complain to me when he starts his old tricks.... Yes, you do. I get it from you on one side and from him on the other, and it makes life hell for me. I'm not going to be the peace-maker anymore. I'm warning you now; when the two of you start fighting again, I'm leaving home.... Mom, if you start crying I'm going to put down the receiver.... Okay.... *(lowering his voice to a vicious whisper)* Okay, Mom. I heard you. *(desperate)* No. Because I don't want to. I'll see him when I get home! Mom! ... *(Pause. When he speaks again his tone changes completely. It is not simply pretense. We sense a genuine emotional conflict.)* Welcome home chum! .... What's that? .... Don't be silly, Dad. You being home is just about the best news in the world..... I bet you are. Bloody depressing there with everybody going on about their ailments, hey!.... How you feeling?... Good.... Here as well, pal. Coming down cats and dogs... *(a weak little laugh)* That's right. Just the day for a kip and a toss in your old Uncle Ned... Everything's just hunky-dory on my side Dad.... Well to start with, there's a nice pile of comics for you on the counter.... Yes, old Kemple brought them in. Batman and Robin, Submariner ... just your cup of tea.... I will.... Yes, we'll spin a few yarns tonight.... Okay chum, see you in a little while.... No, I promise. I'll come straight home.... *(Pause. His mother comes back on the phone.)* Mom? Okay. I'll lock up now.... What?.... Oh, the brandy.... Yes, I'll remember!... I'll put it in my suitcase now, for God's sake. I know well enough what will hapen if he doesn't get it. I was kind to him, Mom. I didn't say anything nasty!... Alright. Bye. *(End of telephone conversation. A desolate HALLY doesn't move. A strained silence.)*

SAM. (quietly) That sounded like a bad bump, Hally.

HALLY. *(Having a hard time controlling his emotions, he speaks carefully.)* Mind your own business, Sam.

SAM. Sorry. I wasn't trying to interfere.... Shall we carry on? Hally? *(He indicates the exercise book.)*

(no response from HALLY)

WILLIE. *(also trying)* Tell him about when they give out the cups, Boet Sam.

SAM. Ja! That's another big moment. The presentation of the cups after the winners have been announced. You've got to put that in.

(still no response from HALLY)

WILLIE. A big silver one, Master Hally, called floating

trophy for the champions.

SAM. We always invite some big-shot personality to hand them over. Guest of houour this year is going to be His Holiness, Bishop Jabulani of the All African Free Zionist Church.

HALLY. *(Gets up abruptly, goes to his table and tears up the page he was writing on.)* So much for a bloody world without collisions.

SAM. Too bad. It was on its way to being a good composition.

HALLY. Let's stop bullshitting ourselves, Sam.

SAM. Have we been doing that?

HALLY. Yes! That's what all our talk about a decent world has been ... just so much bullshit.

SAM. We did say it was still only a dream.

HALLY. And a bloody useless one, at that. Life's a fuck-up and it's never going to change.

SAM. Ja, maybe that's true.

HALLY. There's no maybe about it. It's a blunt and brutal fact. All we've done this afternoon is waste our time.

SAM. Not if we'd got your homework done.

HALLY. I don't give a shit about my homework, so, for Christ's sake, just shut-up about it. *(slamming books viciously into his schoolcase)* Hurry-up now and finish your work. I want to lock-up and get out of here. *(pause)* And then go where? Home-sweet-fucking-home. Jesus, I hate that word.

(SAM and WILLIE work away as unobtrusively as possible.)

HALLY. *(He abandons all further attempts to hide his feelings.)*

Do you want to know what is really wrong with your lovely little dream, Sam? It's not just that we are all bad dancers. That does happen to be perfectly true, but there's more to it than just that. You left out the cripples.

SAM. Hally!

HALLY. *(now totally reckless)* Ja! Can't leave them out, Sam. That's why we always end up on our backsides on the dance-floor. They're also out there dancing ... like a bunch of broken spiders trying to do the quickstep! *(an ugly attempt at laughter)* When you come to think of it, it's a bloody comical sight. I mean it's bad enough on two legs ... but one and a pair of crutches! Hell no, Sam. That's guaranteed to turn that dance floor into a shambles. Why you shaking your head? Picture it, man. For once this afternoon, let's use our imaginations sensibly.

SAM. Be careful, Hally.

HALLY. Of what? The truth? I seem to be the only one around here who is prepared to face it. We've had the pretty dream, it's time now to wake-up and have a good, long look at the way things really are. Nobody knows the steps, there's no music, the cripples are also out there, tripping-up everybody and trying to get into the act and it's all called the All-Comers-How-To-Make-A-Fuckup-Of-Life-Championships. *(another ugly laugh)* Hang-on, Sam! The best bit is still coming. Do you know what the winner's trophy is? A beautiful, big chamber-pot with roses on the side and it's full to the brim with piss. And guess who, I think, is going to be this year's winner?

SAM. *(almost shouting)* Stop now!

HALLY. *(suddenly appalled by how far he has gone)* Why?

SAM. Hally? It's your father you're talking about.

HALLY. So?

SAM. Do you know what you've been saying?

(HALLY can't answer. He is rigid with shame.)

SAM. *(Speaks to him, sternly.)* No, Hally, you mustn't do it. Take back those words and ask forgiveness! It's a terrible sin for a son to mock his father with jokes like that. You'll be punished if you carry on. Your father is your father, even if he is a ... cripple man.

WILLIE. Yes, Master Hally. Is true what Sam say.

SAM. I understand how you are feeling, Hally, but even so....

HALLY. No, you don't!

SAM. I think I do.

HALLY. And I'm telling you, you don't. Nobody does. *(speaking carefully, as his shame turns to rage at SAM)* It's your turn to be careful, Sam. Very careful! You're treading on dangerous ground. Leave me and my father alone.

SAM. I'm not the one who's been saying things about him.

HALLY. What goes on between me and my dad is none of your business!

SAM. Then don't tell me about it. If that's all you've got to say about him, I don't want to hear.

HALLY. *(For a moment he is at a loss for a response.)* Just get on with your bloody work and shut-up.

SAM. Swearing at me won't help you.

HALLY. Yes it does! Mind your own fucking business and shut-up!

SAM. Okay. If that's the way you want it, I'll stop trying.

(He turns away.)

HALLY. *(This infuriates him even more.)* Good. Because what you've been trying to do is meddle in something you know nothing about. All that concerns you in here, Sam, is to try and do what you get paid for — keep the place clean and serve the customers. In plain words, just get on with your job. My mother is right. She's always warning me about allowing you to get too familiar. Well, this time you've gone too far. It's going to stop right now.

(No response from SAM.)

HALLY. You're only a servant in here, and don't forget it.

(Still no response. HALLY is trying hard to get one.)

HALLY. And as far as my father is concerned, all you need to remember is that he is your boss.

SAM. *(needled at last)* No he isn't. I get paid by your mother.

HALLY. Don't argue with me, Sam!

SAM. Then don't say he's my boss.

HALLY. He's a whiteman and that's good enough for you.

SAM. I'll try to forget you said that.

HALLY. Don't! Because you won't be doing me a favour if you do. I'm telling you to remember it.

SAM. *(Pause. Pulls himself together and makes one last effort.)* Hally, Hally...! Come on, now. Let's stop before it's too late. You're right. We *are* on dangerous ground. If we're not careful, somebody is going to get hurt.

HALLY. It won't be me.

SAM. Don't be so sure.

HALLY. I don't know what you're talking about, Sam.

SAM. Yes you do.

HALLY. Jesus, I wish you would stop trying to tell me what I do and what I don't know.

SAM. *(He gives up; turns to WILLIE.)* Let's finish up.

HALLY. Don't turn your back on me! I haven't finished talking. *(He grabs SAM by the arm and tries to make him turn around.)*

SAM. *(Reacts with a flash of anger.)* Don't do that, Hally! *(facing the boy)* Alright, I'm listening. Well? What do you want to say to me?

HALLY. To begin with, why don't you also start calling me Master Harold like Willie.

SAM. Do you mean that?

HALLY. Why the hell do you think I said it?

SAM. And if I don't?

HALLY. You might just lose your job.

SAM. *(quietly and very carefully)* If you make me say it once, I'll never call you anything else again.

HALLY. So? *(The boy confronts the man.)* Is that meant to be a threat?

SAM. Just telling you what will happen if you make me do that. You must decide what it means to you.

HALLY. Well, I have. It's good news. Because that is exactly what Master Harold wants from now on. Think of it as a little lesson in respect, Sam, that's long overdue, and I hope you remember it as well as you do your geography. I can tell you now that somebody who will be glad to hear

I've finally given it to you, will be my dad. Yes! He agrees with my mom. He's always going on about it as well. "You must teach the boys to show you more respect, my son."

SAM. So now you can stop complaining about going home. Everybody is going to be happy tonight.

HALLY. That's perfectly correct. You see, you mustn't get the wrong idea about me and my dad, Sam. We also have our good times together. Some bloody good laughs. He's got a marvellous sense of humour. Want to know what our favourite joke is? He gives out a big groan, you see, and says: "It's not fair, is it, Hally?" Then I have to ask: "What, Chum?" And then he says: "A nigger's arse" ... and we both have a good laugh.

(The men stare at him with disbelief.)

HALLY. What's the matter, Willie? Don't you catch the joke? You always were a bit slow on the up-take. It's what is called a pun. You see, fair means both light in colour and to be just and decent. *(He turns to SAM.)* I thought you would catch it, Sam.

SAM. Oh, Ja, I catch it alright.

HALLY. But it doesn't appeal to your sense of humour.

SAM. Do you really laugh?

HALLY. Of course.

SAM. To please him? Make him feel good?

HALLY. No, for heaven's sake! I laugh because I think it's a bloody good joke.

SAM. You're really trying hard to be ugly, aren't you.

And why drag poor old Willie into it. He's done nothing to you except show you the respect you want so badly. That's also not being fair, you know ... and *I* mean just or decent.

WILLIE. It's alright, Sam. Leave it now.

SAM. It's me you're after. You should just have said, "Sam's arse" ... because that's the one you're trying to kick. Anyway, how do you know it's not fair? You've never seen it. Do you want to? *(He drops his trousers and underpants and presents his backside for Hally's inspection.)* Have a good look... real Basuto arse ... which is about as nigger as they come. Satisfied? *(trousers up)* Now you can make your dad even happier when you go home tonight. Tell him I showed you my arse and he is quite right. It's not fair. And if it will give him an even better laugh next time, I'll also let him have a look. Come, Willie, lets finish up and go.

(SAM and WILLIE start to tidy up the tearoom. HALLY doesn't move. He waits for a moment when SAM passes him.)

HALLY. *(quietly)* Sam...

(SAM stops and looks expectantly at the boy. HALLY spits in his face. A long and heartfelt groan from WILLIE.)

SAM. *(For a few seconds he doesn't move. He takes out a handkerchief and wipes his face.)* It's alright, Willie. *(to HALLY)* Ja, well, you've done it ... Master Harold. Yes, I'll start calling you that from now on. It won't be difficult anymore. You've hurt yourself, Master Harold. I saw it coming. I warned you, but you wouldn't listen. You've just hurt yourself *bad*. And you're a coward, Master Howard. The face you should be spitting in is your father's ... but you used mine, because you think you're safe inside your fair skin ... and this time I don't mean just or decent. *(pause)* Should I hit him, Willie?

WILLIE. No, Boet Sam.

SAM. *(violently)* Why not?

WILLIE. It won't help, Boet sam.

SAM. I don't want to help! I want to hurt him.

WILLIE. You also hurt yourself.

SAM. And if he had done it to you, Willie?

WILLIE. Me? Spit at me like I was a dog? *(A thought that had not occurred to him before. He looks at HALLY.)* Ja. Then I want to hit him. I want to hit him hard!

(A dangerous few seconds as the men stand staring at the boy.)

WILLIE. *(Turns away, shaking his head.)* But maybe all I do is go cry at the back. He's little boy, Boet Sam. Little *white* boy. Long trousers now, but he's still little boy.

SAM. *(his violence ebbing away into defeat as quickly as it flooded)* You're right. So go on then; groan again, Willie. You do it better than me. *(to HALLY)* You don't know all of what you've just done, ... Master Harold. It's not just that you've made me feel dirtier than I've ever been in my life ... I mean, how do I wash off your and your father's filth? ... I've also failed. A long time ago I promised myself I was going to try and do something, but you've just shown me ... Master Harold ... that I've failed. *(pause)* I've also got a memory of a little white boy when he was still wearing short trousers and a black man, but they're not flying a kite. It was the old Jubilee days, after dinner one night. I was in my room. You came in and just stood against the wall, looking down at the ground, and only after I'd asked you what you wanted, what was wrong, I don't know how many times, did you speak and even then, so softly I almost didn't hear you. "Sam, please help me to go and fetch my dad." Remember? He was dead drunk on the floor of the Central Hotel Bar. They'd phoned for your mom, but you were the only one at home. And do you remember how we did it? You went in first, by yourself, to ask permission for me to go into the bar. Then I loaded him onto my back like a baby and carried him back to the boarding house with you following behind, carrying his crutches. *(shaking his head as he remembers)* A crowded Main Street with all the people watching a little white boy following his drunk father on a nigger's back! I felt for that little boy... Master Harold. I felt for him. After that we still had to clean him up, remember. He'd messed in his trousers, so we had to clean him up and get him into bed.

HALLY. *(great pain)* Sam, I love him.

SAM. I know you do. That's why I tried to stop you from saying these things about him. It would have been so simple if you could have just despised him for being a weak man. But he's your father. You love him and you're ashamed of him. You're ashamed of so much!... and now that's going to include yourself. That was the promise I made to myself: to try and stop that happening. *(pause)* After we got him in bed you came back with me to my room and sat in a corner and carried on just looking down at the ground. And for days after that! You hadn't done anything wrong but you went around as if you owed the world an apology for being alive. I didn't like seeing that! That's not the way a boy grows up to be a man! ... But the one person who should have been teaching you what that means was the cause of your shame. If you really want to know, that's why I made you that kite. I wanted you to look up, be proud of something, of yourself ... *(bitter smile at the memory)* ... and you certainly were that, when I left you with it up there on the hill. Oh ja ... something else! ... If you ever do write it as a short story there *was* a twist in our ending. I couldn't sit down there and stay with you. It was a whites-only bench. You were too young, too excited, to notice then. But not anymore. If you're not careful ... Master Harold ... you're going to be sitting up there by yourself for a long time to come, and there won't be a kite in the sky. *(He has nothing more to say. He exits into the kitchen, taking off his waiter's jacket.)*

WILLIE. Is bad. Is all, all bad in here now.

HALLY. *(books into his suitcase, raincoat on)* Willie ... *(It is difficult to speak.)* Will you lock up for me and look after the keys?

WILLIE. Okay.

(SAM returns. HALLY goes behind the counter and collects the few coins in the cash register. As he starts to leave:)

SAM. Don't forget the comic books.

(HALLY returns to the counter and puts them in his case. He starts to leave again.)

SAM. *(to the retreating back of the boy)* Stop.

(HALLY stops but doesn't turn to face him.)

SAM. Hally ... I've got no right to tell you what being a man means if I don't behave like one myself, and I'm not doing so well at that this afternoon. Should we try again, Hally?

HALLY. Try what?

SAM. Fly another kite, I suppose. It worked once, and this time I need it as much as you do.

HALLY. It's still raining, Sam. You can't fly kites on rainy days, remember?

SAM. So what do we do? Hope for better weather tomorrow?

HALLY. *(helpless gesture)* I don't know. I don't know anything anymore.

SAM. You sure of that, Hally? Because it would be pretty hopeless if that was true. It would mean nothing has been learnt in here this afternoon, and there was a hell of a lot of teaching going on ... one way or the other. But anyway, I don't believe you. I reckon there's one thing you know. You don't *have* to sit up there by yourself. You know what that bench means now, and you can leave it any time you choose. All you've got to do is stand up, and walk away from it. *(He leaves.)*

WILLIE. *(Goes up, quietly, to SAM.)* Is okay, Boet Sam. You see. Is ... *(He can't find any better words.)* ... is going to be okay tomorrow. *(changing his tone)* Hey, Boet Sam! *(He is trying hard.)* You right. I think about it and you right. Tonight I find Hilda and say sorry. And make promise I won't beat her no more. You hear me, Boet Sam?

SAM. I hear you, Willie.

WILLIE. And when we practice, I relax and romance with her from beginning to end. Non-stop! You watch! Two weeks' time: First Prize For Promising New-comers: Mr. Willie Malopo and Miss Hilda Samules. *(sudden impulse)* To hell with it; I walk home. *(He goes to the jukebox, puts in a coin and selects a record. The machine comes to life in the grey twilight, blushing its way through a spectrum of soft, romantic colours.)* How did you say it, Boet Sam? Let's dream. *(Presenting himself as a partner.)*

(The jukebox plays.)
LITTLE MAN YOU'RE CRYING,
I KNOW WHY YOU'RE BLUE.
SOMEONE TOOK YOUR KIDDY-CAR AWAY.
A' BETTER GO TO SLEEP NOW;
LITTLE MAN, YOU'VE HAD A BUSY DAY.

WILLIE. You lead, I follow.

(The jukebox plays.)
JOHNNY WON YOUR MARBLES. TELL YOU WHAT WE'LL DO.
DAD WILL GET YOU NEW ONES RIGHT AWAY.
BETTER GO TO SLEEP NOW;
LITTLE MAN, YOU'VE HAD A BUSY DAY.
etc. etc. The men dance together.)

END OF PLAY

PROPERTIES
TOP OF SHOW PRESET

OFF-LEFT:
*Schoolcase w/
    Zane Grey book (bookmark — random)
    Math book
    History book
    Dictionary
    Notebook (top right corner folded slightly forward)
    Ruler
    Pencil case w/
        Pen, 2 pencils (sharpened) pencil sharpener
*Tray w/
    Bowl of pea soup
    Cloth
*Cloth
*Towel (on hook by kitchen door)
Extra bowl of soup

ON STAGE:
Front counter:
    Cash register (no sale up)
    *Three shillings (in cash register)
    Candy jar filled with red licorice
    *Cake stand w/ 2 blueberry muffins & 2 Twinkie halves

*Needs to be preset each performance.

Telephone
Rubber stamp
Ink pad
*Waiter's pad (clean sheet each show)
Pencil
Side dish of toothpicks

Freezer:
  *Chest of ice
  *Vanilla ice-cream
  *Bottle of ginger-ale
On top of freezer:
  *Tablecloth
  Ice-cream scoop
Top downstage shelf:
  *Bottle of brandy (extra bottle of brandy)
  *Ice-cream spoon
  *Spare ice-cream scoop
Second upstage shelf:
  *Tray
Back counter:
  Coffee urn
  6 coffee cups
  *Plate
  *Knife, fork and spoon
  Salt & pepper shakers
  *Napkin
  *Cloth
*Sugar dispenser w/sugar
*Water pitcher, covered w/ napkin

*Needs to be preset each performance.

Glass shelves:
  4 soda bottles (top)
  Cigarette display (middle)
  Candy display (middle)
Underneath back counter:
  *5 tablecloths (US top shelf)
  12 napkins (US bottom shelf)
  Soup bowl, 3 side plates, tea cup (center top shelf)
  4 plates (center top shelf)
  2 plates (center shelf)
  *Glasses including ice-cream soda glass (DS top shelf)
Ice-cream glasses (DS Bottom shelf)
Towel rack w/
  2 gold bordered towels
*White trash can (by US end of back counter — preset
    with pane of glass)
Waiter's hat (3rd hook)
Waiter's jacket (4th hook)
*6 tables
*12 chairs
*5 comic books (DR table)
*Red bordered cloth (DR table)
*Bucket (⅓ filled with warm water)
*Rag (in bucket)
*Flat cardboard box
*6 ashtrays (UC table) *6 empty sugar bowls (UC table)
Broom (UL corner)
Dust pan (UL corner)
Fern in large blue pot (DR of jukebox)

*Needs to be preset each performance.

Blue pot with long-leafed plant (SR window sill)
Cardboard sign (SR window sill)
Shell dish (SR window sill)
Red, round pot w/ dead plant (SR window sill)
Blue pitcher w/ plant (C window sill)
Orange pot w/ plant (C window sill)
Light blue, long pot w/ plant (SL window sill)
Red, narrow vase (SL window sill)
Cadbury sign (over jukebox)
Coke sign (back wall)
Calender [June] (above coffee urn)
Menu (above back counter)
Proud service sign (US of kitchen door)
*Light switch (down position)
*Curtains (all opened)
*Doors closed

PERSONAL

Quarter (WILLIE)

*Needs to be preset each performance.

RUNNING PROPS AND PERISHABLES

PERISHABLES:

Red Licorice
Ginger-ale
Vanilla ice-cream
Blueberry muffins (1 eaten per show)
Twinkies (½ eaten per show)
Pea soup (1 cup eaten per show)
Ice

RUNNING PROPS:
Bottle caps
Panes of glass (1 broken per show)
Hot pot (to make soup in)
Funnel (for filling the ginger-ale bottle)

TOP OF SHOW COSTUME PRESET

OFF LEFT:

Sam's sports jacket, tie
Sam's hat
Willie's out door jacket
Willie's hat

Kite
→ to detraumatize
Hally

COSTUME PLOT

SAM:
Black pleated pants
Long-sleeved, button-down white shirt
Waiter's jacket
Black belt
Black socks
Boxer shorts
Shiny, burgundy oxford shoes
Undershirt (optional)
Watch — leather strap
Black bow tie
(Sports jacket)
(Hat)
(Striped regular tie)

WILLIE:
Gray pleated pants
Long-sleeved, button-down white shirt
Belt
White kitchen apron
White sweat socks
Black work boots
Boxer shorts
Black bow tie
(Blue jacket)
(Straw hat)

Animal Farm